LIFE CHANGING THOUGHTS

"GOOD THOUGHTS ARE LIKE TREASURE OF INNER PEACE & HAPPINESS"

RANJAN KUMAR THAPA

<u>**ABOUT THE AUTHOR**</u>

Ranjan Kumar Thapa is a teacher and a motivational speaker, who lives with his family in India(West Bengal, Darjeeling). He is the founder of "MRK Publicatons" and also owns Educational institute and Motivational show especially for students, his motto is "Good Thoughts Good Life." Apart from teaching he also guides the students in developing their personality. He always had a passion for writing book to illuminate the path of the students so that they can be motivated and guided to choose the right path. He enjoys spending time in the lap of nature for refreshment.

Keep in touch with Ranjan Kumar Thapa via the social media:

Facebook: Rk Thapa Jr.(MRK Publications)

Instagram: mrk.publications_sainikpuri_21

Office No. 8116782587

Contents

Foreword — vii

Preface — ix

Acknowledgements — xi

Prologue — xiii

1. Thoughts Of Ranjan Kumar Thapa — 1

2. Thoughts Of Students — 8

3. Thoughts Of Teachers — 16

4. Special Message — 24

Foreword

Life Changing thoughts is a collection of thoughts and messages from peoples, teachers and students.
This book is a must read for the one who wants to lead a successful life. It has a wonderful content that will enhance and help you polish your skills
to move forward in your career with confidence and positivity.
The book is helpful in fostering following qualities in you:
*Confidence
*Self -awareness
*Courage
*Respect
*Gratitude
*Patience
*Open mindedness
*Broader Vision of Life.
The book is a result of lots of research and hard work, done for the personal development of the reader.
"Positive thinking is the first step towards happiness to overcome problems and get away from negativity".
-Ranjan Kumar Thapa

Preface

Take a step closer to "POSITIVITY", by allowing yourself to be guided by this treasure trove of thoughts, coming directly from the hearts and minds of people around you to inspire and motivate you throughout the journey of your life. This book is about the positive thoughts and message of teachers, students and people from different profession. I hope this thought will motivate you to overcome your difficulties and challenges in your life.

This book is dedicated to my father Late. Shri Sukh Kumar Thapa and my mother Smt. Renu Kumari Thapa whose inspiration and support always meant a lot.

Special Thanks to all the teachers and students for collaborating with me in this small initiative of spreading Positivity.

Special Thanks to Ms. Bandana Biswakarma for editing the thoughts and special messages.

-Ranjan kumar Thapa
M.Sc. B.Ed
Founder Of MRK Publications

Acknowledgements

MRK Publications, TCP More, Sainikpuri(Khaprail bazar), Matigara, Darjeeling(W.B), Siliguri-734009, email: infomrkpublications@gmail.com, contact no. 8116782587

Prologue

SKYLARK EDUCATIONAL TRUST, TCP Road, Sainikpuri, Gurukripa, Matigara, darjeeling(W.B), Siliguri-734009, email: info.skylarktrust@gmail.com, web: www.skylarktrust.in, office no. +91 7908972025

THOUGHTS OF RANJAN KUMAR THAPA

POSITIVE THINKING IS THE FIRST STEP TOWARDS HAPPINESS TO OVERCOME PROBLEMS. SO, MAKE SPACE FOR POSITIVITY AND GET AWAY FROM NEGATIVITY.
- Ranjan Kumar Thapa

- Start your own enterprise,

  as job has possibility of replacement.

- Two things exist in this world NATURALISTIC & MATERIALISTICS,

  one must choose wisely whom to love.

- Thoughts are the key to explore the universe,

  GOOD THOUGHTS and BAD THOUGHTS
  might explore SINFULNESS.

- Never FORGETS two great teachers of life,

  SUCCESS and FAILURE both have
  their own ways of TEACHING.

- FOCUS on what you have

  rather than LAMENTAING over
  what you have LOST.

- What I am today might not be TOMORROW,

  as everyday learning leads to CHANGE for BETTER.

- TRUST is like a flower,

  which takes time to BLOOM,
  but gets WITHERED away if BROKEN.

- TRUE friends are BLESSING for life and

  FAKE friends are TEACHING for LIFE.

- Having ENEMIES to CRTICIZE is better than having

  FAKE friends as CRITICISM leads to IMPROVEMENT.

- OVERTHINKING is not a PROBLEM

  if you do it might give ways to MIRACLES.

- Never HURT anyone and

  don't get HURT by ANYONE.

- REJECTION or NEGLIGENCE doesn't matter

  when you RISE above these.

- Working to uplift your life might be ADVENTURES,

  but the will to uplift others
  along with you is COURAGEOUS.

- SOMETIMES best comes out of WORST SITUATION,

  so don't GIVE UP and KEEP CONTINUING

- The BEST wish to be asked in PRAYERS

  is to PRAY GOD to be in your MIND & HEART.

- LOSING everything doesn't matter,

  what matters more is to have
  FAITH & BELIEVE in GOD.
  BELIEVE me you can do
  all that you want just be HONEST
  to your DREAMS and put the
  EFFORT PURELY & WHOLE heartedly.

- LOVE is not what we see and try to IMITATE from movies.

  LOVE is that DIVINE TRUTH which is PORTAYARD in the
  LOVE story of RADHA KRISHNA. Which will always
  Remain alive in our HEARTS.

- If you really want to SUCCEED

  in life then FOCUS on your DREAMS and

LEARN from your FAILURES.

- Most effective and BRAIN BOOSTING

  techniques is to THINK POSITIVE
  in RIGHT DIRECTION.

- SUCCESS depends on the EFFORT

  you make to ENHANCES your CAPABLITIES.

- GOD has created EVERYONE

  with UNIQUENESS and this DIVERSITY
  should be APPRECIATED.

- NEVER indulge yourself on SUCCESS and FAILURES,

  rather enjoy every bit of the JOURNEY called LIFE.

- BEST habits you can include in 2021-22 is to

  TURN OFF your MOBILE PHONE one hour before you go to SLEEP
  to avoid UNNECESSARY LOAD on YOUR MIND.

- The BEST time to START working

  on your DREAM is RIGHT NOW.

- MIND & HEART are the PLACE

  where POSITIVE THOUGHTS grow.
  So, PROTECT it from NEGATIVE THOUGHTS
  & UNPLEASENT DESIRES.

- EVERY child has the POTENTIAL

  to do great deeds but LACK of CONSISTENCY
  lead them away from their GOAL.

- BE CAUTIOUS of your thoughts and words

  as these DECIDE your JOURNEY of LIFE.

- Its DIFFCULT to get a person

  who cares about you in this BUSY WORLD.
  So, if you find one don't let that PERSON go.

- Not being both with EXTRAORDINARY TALENT is OKAY.

  Just be KIND to everyone, and do a small act of KINDNESS
  that WILL make your LIFE EXTRAORDINARY.

- When STUDIES get TIRING don't give up.

  Just CHANGE the strategy and feel the differences
  and NEVER GIVE UP.

- PURE mind, HEALTHY body and GREAT GOALS

  are perfect COMBINATION for living life to its FULLEST.

- When we understand the

  CAUSE of ATTACHMENT in our LIFE.
  We should not be DISAPPOINTED
  with ANYONE or ANYTHING.

- PHYSICAL beauty ENHANCES PRIDE, JEALOUSLY & DIFFRENCES

  among others and ENDS one day but INNER beauty ENHANCES PEACE, LOVE, ENLIGHTMENT and stays alive in the MIND & HEART FOREVER.

- PATIENCES is STRONGEST

  Bridge between your TRUE EFFORT and ULTIMATE SUCCESS.

- If you want to LIVE LONG stay

  TUNED and CONNECTED to NATURE. NATURE heals INTOXICATION PURIFYING your BODY & MIND.

- IF you are not HAPPY

  it MEANS you are in WRONG place.

- ADVERSITIES open up your EYES and

  IMPARTS true values of LIFE.

- GOOD THOUGHTS are like

  TREASURE of INNER PEACE & HAPPINESS.

- BELIEVE in yourself,

  you are BORN TO WIN.
  Just move don't STOP.

- A person without a VISION in his LIFE,

  is like a DIRECTION less KITE in the SKY.

- There are lots of OPTIONS

  for us to CHOOSE from, so CHOOSE wisely as
  WRONG choice might cause DISPARITY.

- Use TECHNOLOGY wisely,

  be the MASTER of TECHNOLOGY,
  DON'T let TECHNOLOGY be your MASTER.

CHAPTER TWO

THOUGHTS OF STUDENTS

Muskan Jha. XII Vocational
Poet
PurbaMadati Jayantika Tea Estate
*NOTHING can STOP a DESIRING
heart from ACHIEVING SUCCESS.*

****

-Anindita Sarkar, Class :11 'Humanities'
Regional/State Level winner and National Level Science
Exhibition Participant 2019.
BAGDOGRA (Dist: Darjeeling, WEST BENGAL)
*COOPERATION is just like our two FEET,
it's EASIER to walk with both,
TOUGHER to walk with one and
IMPOSSIBLE to walk with NONE.
* When the world is AGAINST you but
you know your PURPOSE to FIGHT is TRUE and LEGIT,
hold on to your CONFIDENCE and March FORWARD,
VICTORY will be yours.
* When we CLENCH our fist tight enough,
to not let our POSITIVITY and PEACE of mind
spill out into the outer world of APATHY and NEGATIVITY,
only then we can termed to be TRULY POWERFUL.

*If you WISH to WIN try to COMPETE
but if you NEED to WIN then
FIGHT to COMPETE.
*Falling of the PETALS is not the END
it is the BEGINNING of a
NEW FRUITING SESSION.
*A CANDLES LIGHT can show you the PATH
to move but only LIGHT OF KNOWLEDGE
can give you the COURAGE to STEP FORWARD
on that PATH.
*WORDS are the JEWELS to every THOUGHT.
****

-*Shubhadip Majumdar, Class: 9 C,*
Daspara, Chopra, Uttar Dinajpur(West Bengal)

*TEACHER is a guide to show you the PATH. But you are the ONE to walk through it.

*DIFFICULTIES are the CHECKPOINTS of the LIFE. They are not let you down, but to TEST your STRENGTHS and WEAKNESS, So that you can know your LIMITS

*KNOWLWDGE is EVERYWHWERE, it is like the ENDLESS UNIVERSE. You just NEED how to ACQUIRE it.

*Never try to MEMORIZE, try to UNDERSTAND, as UNDERSTANDING lasts LONGER.

*SEARCH for a TEACHER in your LIFE, who will know you as his BEST FRIEND, and who will always stand behind you. The day when you will find such a TEACHER, you will be the richest PERSON of the UNIVERSE.
****

-*Mayuri Churiwal, Class: IX C*
Pink Town House, Gurugram (Haryana)
Poetries publish in book(Flames of imagination and Bad faith buddy)

*RESPONSIBITY is not only about growing yourself as an UNIQUE IDEAL, but also helping the WORLD grow as SPECTRUM where UNITY is strength and INDIVIDUALITY is

EXTOLLED.

*EVERYONE can LOVE YOU because of your BEAUTIFUL FACE, but find SOMEONE who can LOVE you even in the HALLOWEEN night where SPECIAL FACE doesn't get a CHANCE to define the BEAUTY.

*GOD is great ARTIST who used different colours to PAINT our SKIN. SOMETIMES he felt like using WHITE, sometimes BLACK and sometimes BROWN. EVERY colour he uses is ATTRACTIVE so the Hell are the PEOPLE to practice racism?

*PEACE is that medicine which HEALS the broken SOUL and MIND with ease. It is a STRONG IMMUNITY BOOSTER that fights all NEGATIVITY and NAUSEOUS THOUGHTS.

*You don't become COOL by wearing fancy clothes or shoes. Wearing a SENSIBLE PERSONALITY can do it all.

*SITUATION have not SIGNED any AGREEMENT with you that they will give everything you DESIRE. So be READY for every worst that comes over and do not COMPLAIN but take ACTIONS according to your SITUATIONS.

****

-Shah Ziya, Class-10
Chopra, Uttar Dinajpur (West Bengal)

*SOMETIMES just take a moment to APPRECIATE yourself because you need MOTIVATION too.

*TEARS are not something that show how WEAK or STRONG one is. They are just one's EMOTTIONS that they could no longer hold in.

*To HELP someone is your CHOICE. But you have got no RIGHT HURT.

-Kaushik Kanon Saha Das, Class: Student in Aakash Institution, Siliguri
Shivmandir, Near B.ED college(West Bengal, Distt: Darjeeling (siliguri)

*It doesn't matter, where you BELONG to.
What matter is, where you bring
your BELONGONGS to.

****

-Kewal Rai, year: 2ndyear (Tycoons International)
Darjeeling (West Bengal)
*If you want to ACHIEVE something in LIFE,
start IMAGINING as it is the
PREVIEW of what you want to ACHIEVE.
****

-Priya Thakur, 2ndyear, B.Sc program (Siliguri College)
Khaprail, Sainikpuri (West Bengal, Darjeeling)
*Saying YES to YOURSELF
is the first step that takes you
CLOSER to your AIM.
*PEOPLE striving for SUCCESS
do not have EXCUSES but the strong
INTENSTIONS and DETERMINATION.
-Subham Chhetri B.Com (Birpara College)
Birpara, Alipurduar district (West Bengal)
*LIFE is like water cycle,
EVERYONE when you are ELATED,
CONDENSATION when you are
MELANCHOLY and PRECIPITATION
when you are TRAGICOMIC.
*LEARNING is an ART and you are an ARTIST,
Keep belief like a PRIEST but don't fold your wrist,
just OPEN your MIND and use your fist.
-Prayoshi Roy, Class: VIII C
Ghoshpukur, Kamala Tea Garden (West Bengal, Darjeeling)
*The first CHALLENGE of our LIFE is to
TRUST and BELIEVE ourselves,
as it DECIDES what our DESTINY holds for us.
*FAMILY wraps the BEST GIFT of our life
''OUR PARENTS'', with whose HELP
we can OVERCOME any DIFFICULTIES.
*TRUST is a SMALL word,
it takes a second to PRONOUNCE,

a minute to understand,

and a day to THINK but whole life to PROVE it.

*MOM is a SOLUTION of every problem in your LIFE. When you face problems in your life just go and HUG her TIGHTLY and SAY ''ALWAYS BE WITH ME'' and see the MIRCLE.

****

-Kritika Thapa, Class: 11 Arts

Grassmore Tea garden (West Bengal, Darjeeling)

*You can do it,

whatever you are TRYING to do.

So, don't lose HOPE.

****

-Aparna Das Modak , Class: X A

Mailani Jote, Kamala Bagan (West Bengal, Darjeeling)

*FAILURES doesn't define you as weak,

instead these make you STRONGER

to GROW and ACHIEVE more.

****

-Prathana Thapa, Class: 9 A (Fulbari, Siliguri)

Durga Mandir, Towerline Near Rani House, Shivmandir (West Bengal, Darjeeling)

*Don't give up and give your BEST,

until you become a SUCCESSFUL PEOPLE.

*To be BEAUTIFUL means to be YOURSELF,

you don't have to be ACCEPTED by others,

you have to ACCEPT yourself FIRST.

*Your HARD WORK will bear

fruit keep on WORKING.

*one day SOMEONE will live

you the way you DESERVED to be LOVED,

you don't have to fight for it.

****

-Mani Ranjan, Class: 10(Vidyamandir Classes, Patna)

Gogri, Jamalpur, District: Khagaria(Bihar)

*Don't think too much about LIFE,

the LIFE GIVER has PREDEFINED your DESTINY.
*When your PARENTS
want you to do SOMETHING do it,
as your PARENTS always want
BEST for you.
****

-Dristi Sharma, Class: 11 Arts (Siliguri)
Milan More, Champasari, Siliguri(Distt; Darjeeling, WB)
*You learn more from FAILURE
than from SUCCESS,
don't let it STOP your JOURNEY.
*FAILURE can NEVER OVERTAKE
us if our DETERMINATION
to SUCCESS is STRONG.
*FEAR is an ILLOGICAL
feeling that BLOCKS our LOGICAL THINKING so,
take the RISK and consult your PARENTS.
*LIFE'S not easy once you've
the DESIRED to DEAL with your
CHALLENGES but, it's better than GIVING UP.
****

-Ananya Sinha, Class: 10 A (Bidhannagar, Madati)
Bidhannagar, Vivekananda Pally (Distt: Darjeeling, West
Bengal)
*it's your LIFE never depend on OTHERS,
lead it as you LIKE.
*Keep TRYING until you
REACH the GOAL, never ever GIVE UP.
*TIME once wasted never RETUNRS BACK,
so UTILIZE it WISELY.
*LIFE is full of ADVENTURES
face the OBSTACLES and
WIN OVER THEM.
****

-Nausheen Khan, Class: IX A (Bidhannagar, Madati)

Alimganj, PO: Madati, Distt: Darjeeling (West Bengal.
*THINK good and
good will FIND YOU.
****

-Cathrin Joshi, B.A 2nd year (Siliguri College)
Painikumari, Distt: Darjeeling (West Bengal)
*Even if you are in the DARK
create your own RAY OF HOPE.
*In every SITUATION remember
to keep your STRONGEST weapons with you,
''KINDNESS AND SMILE''.
*There are many waiting outside
to call you WRONG, BAD, UNFAITHFUL,
so never give up MOTIVATING YOURSELF.
****

-Rimi Roy, Class: IX A (Bidhan nagar, Madati)
Paikpara, Distt: Darjeeling (West Bengal)
*Positive thinking does not GUARANTEE success,
POSITIVE THINKING with POSITIVE EFFORTS does.
*START each day with a NEW HOPE,
and BELIEVE in the BETTER TOMORROW.
*You are a WRITER of your own story
so write SOMETHING GOOD EVERYDAY.
*EVALUATE to ACCESS something positive
so that you can get POSITIVE RESULTS.
*STOP being AFRAID of what can go WRONG and
START being POSITIVE about
what can go RIGHT.
****

-Aniket Jaiswal, Class: IX B (Bidhannagar, Madati)
Khoribari, Fullbarjote, Distt: Darjeeling (West Bengal)
*EVERYTHING is possible
when you are SURROUNDED
by the RIGHT PEOPLE.
*Your IMMUNITY is your RIGHT,

society's IMMUNITY is your DUTY.
*To have PEOPLE ''ATTITUDE '' is GOOD,
but it SHOULD be POSITIVE.
*If not BEST try to be BETTER.
****

-*Sabri Ashrafa, Class: IX C (Bidhannagar, Madati)*
Sonapur, Uttar Dinajpur (Darjeeling, West Bengal)
*SELF-CONFIDENCE is the
FIRST STEP towards SUCCESS.
****

Lalitesh Prasad Sinha, XII Commerce
Church More, Gayaganga (Darjeeling, West Bengal)
*Utilising time with friends will
Give you beautiful MEMORIES.
But UTILISING time on YOOURSEF
Will give you BEAUTIFUL future
MEMORIES.

CHAPTER THREE

THOUGHTS OF TEACHERS

-Pritam Rai, M.A, B.Ed
Ghayabari, Kurseong (Darjeeling, West Bengal)
*"LIFE is all about POSSIBILITIES
so NEVER GIVE UP".
*"Self BELIEVE is the only
PATH to achieve SUCCESS".
*"Never say I CAN'T ALWAYS
keep NEVER GIVING UP attitude.
*"LIFE is like a RAINBOW
and it becomes colourful only when
we have problems and their SOLUTIONS".
*"TEAM WORK is the GREATEST WEAPON
in bringing the CHANGE".
*"MISTAKES give you the
GREATEST lesson in LIFE".
*"COMPARISON makes you feel inferior,
so never compare yourself to OTHERS".
****

-Payel Agarwal, M.A(English Literature)
Siliguri(Darjeeling, West Bengal)
*"CRITICISM makes
one a better person".

*"FAILURE is the FIRST
step to SUCCESS".
*"NEVER give up on your DREAMS.
Keep trying, even if you have
FAILED ONCE, TWICE or THRICE".
*"ALWAYS have a POSITIVE ATTITUDE towards life,
one positive THOUGHT
can CHANGE the way you live YOUR LIFE".
*"BREAK the FETTERS that CAGE
your wings like a PHOENIX,
RISE from the ASHES and spread your WINGS,
fly high to fulfil your BROKEN DREAMS".
****

*-Piya Jhilmil Chakraborty, M.A(English lit. and language),
Darjeeling Govt. College
Baranilpur, Burdwan, West Bengal*
*"SUCCESS stories may give you INSPIRATION but FAILURE
stories will give you CREDIBILITY".
*"UNTIL you LOVE and RESPECT your PARENTS,
you can't be LOVED and RESPECTED in LIFE".
*"What you read in your CHILDHOOD
will make you the MAN OF TOMORROW.
So, CHOOSE and READ wisely".
*"DO not FORGET to FUEL
the URGE within you REGULARLY,
Because that's what helps you to be in FUTURE".
****

*-Shampa Mukherjee, BA(English HONS),
TTC PG Diploma in Journalism, Co-Ordinator Primary Wings.
60B Raja Dinendra Street, Kolkatta (West Bengal)*
*"Don't push yourself to an extent
where you forget WHO YOU ARE"
*"THOUGHTS are like MAGNETS.
If you THINK POSITIVE, POSITIVITY fills in.
If you THINK NEGATIVE, NEGATIVITY flows in".

*"NOURISH your SOUL
as you NOURISH YOUR BODY".
*"LIVE a simple LIFE to UNDERSATND
what is PEACE and JOY".
*"If you SPEAK behind others
ask yourself, "AM I PERFECT"?
*"When you LOVE a PERSON,
LOVE as you LOVE YOURSELF,
don't look for FAULTS".
*"TRUDE LOVE keeps no EXPECTAIONS".
*"Still you MIND for few SECONDS,
you can hear your INNER VOICE".
*"SOLUTIONS help you to MOVE FORWARD,
WORRIES makes you STAGNANT''.
****

-Ashish Kumar Saha, M.Com, B.Ed
Kishanganj, Bihar
*"ENORMITY of DANGER doesn't matter
what matters is the COURAGE of SELF BELIEF".
*INNER STRENGTH decides whether
the danger was DANGEROUS or it JUST seemed
DANGEROUS".
*"ROOT of the tree will decide whether
THREAT was REAL OR HOAX".
****

*"FOCUSING on PROBLEMS, create more PROBLEMS,
FOCUSING on POSSIBILITIES create more OPPORTUNITIES".
-Kripasindhu, M.A, B.Ed
Padampur, Distt- Bargarh, Odisha
*"Don't be AFRAID if LIFE pushes you BACK, because LIFE is
PREPARING you to JUMP FORWARD".
-Kripasindhu, M.A, B.Ed
Padampur, Distt- Bargarh, Odisha
****

-Darshana Chettri, BA(English Hons.), B.Ed

Salugara, Siliguri (Darjeeling, West Bengal)
*"Always BELIEVE in the POWER of TRUTH,
it might be PAINFUL but at the END of the
DAY it's worth it".
*"If you FAIL, set yourself FRE,
let your HEART spread it's WORTH it'.
*"YOU are NEVER too LATE to begin MY FRIEND".
*"NO one can pull you down,
when you are BORN TO SHINE".
*"STAND on your own, and find the way.
*"SOME nights will be filled with TEARS,
But there's definitely a NEW DAY''.
*"SET your GOALS,
Don't be SCARED to FIGHT,
It's time to OPEN UP.
Things from it is ALWAYS BETTER".
*"LIVE your own LIFE.
No one CAN COMPETE with you on being YOU''.
*"Every child is like a FLOWER of different colour,
different size and different fragrance
but looks BEAUTIFUL when BLOOMED".
*"Always look at the SUNNY side of EVERYTHING,
Your OPTIMISM will come TRUE".
*"Let us PAINT the FINGERS more to be
CREATIVE and POINT the FINGERS less".
*"HAPPINESS lies when you do your part with FULL
DEVOTION,
Rather than doing things out of COMPULSION".
*"A classroom with students is like a FRUIT SALAD,
TASTES different but gives Sweetness.
And, TEACHERS are like the JUICER,
that SQUEEZES those FRUITS and
BRINGS out the BEST of it".
****
-Sujit Sharma, M.Sc(Chemistry Hons)

Samastipur, Bihar.
*"Our ABILITY is not DECIDED by the things we don't know,
Rather it DEPENDS on our FINDING to know the
UNKNOWN".
*"SUCCESS comes to those
Whose CONTINUOUSLY ADHERES to HARD WORK".
*"EVERY failure gives you
ANOTHER chance to WORK HARD
So, never FALL BEHIND".
****

-Deetsha Roy Choudhary, M.A, B.Ed
South Bharat Nagar, Jalpaiguri (West Bengal)
*"Let's just simply ENJOY the TWIST and TURNS,
slopes and ELEVATION in our LIFE to ENJOY and
attain the TRUE HAPPINESS".
****

-Barkha Lama, M.A(Sociology)
Shivmandir, Siliguri, Darjeeling (West Bengal)
*"WORRIES are WASTE of TIME,
CHANGES nothing rather messes with
Our MIND and STEALS our HAPPINESS".
****

*-Prashant Chettri, PGT(Computer Sciences & Informatics
practices)*
Upper Gandhi Nagar, Siliguri (Darjeeling, West Bengal)
*"There is NO PERFECT time to be READY
than the time when you get an OPPORTUNITY.
It is the moment you are READY''.
*"Let's eliminate the
DARKNESS within and in others
With the GOOD INSIDE US.
*"Let's keep up the flame with the ETERNAL FUEL
that we are TRULY BLESSED WITH".
****

-Roshini Jaiswal, M.Sc, B.Ed

Khoribari, Darjeeling (West Bengal)
*"Don't make PERMANENT
Decisions on TEMPORARY
FEELINGS".
****

-Swastika Bardewa, M.A(Political Science, Kalipada Ghosh Terai mahavidyalaya)

Sanyasi More near Medical More, Shivmandir(Darjeeling, West Bengal)

*"WAKE UP with DETERMINATION.
Go to bed with SATISFACTION".
*"You are CAPABLE of doing AMAZING THINGS".
*"STUDY HARD students you may get
DARK CIRCLES because of not GETTING
Proper sleep but one day you will get
REWARDED for the HARD WORK".
*"PUSH yourself to the EDGE,
check your limits,
See what are you limits, see
What are you CAPABLE OF,
SUFFER, SACRIFICE and WIN".
*"The GREATEST sin is to THINK yourself WEAK".
*"Failure is OPPORTUNITY
to begin MORE INTELLIGENTLY".
*"FAILURE is the OPPRTUNITY to
Begin again more INTELLIGRNTLY".

-Swastika Bardewa, M.A(Political Science, Kalipada Ghosh Terai mahavidalaya)

Sanyasi More near Medical More, Shivmandir(Darjeeling, West Bengal)

****

Mandira Rai, M.A(Nepali) , B.Ed
Panchandi Dgapur
*"REAL AVENGERS are those
who has the will to CHANGE NEGATIVITY to

POSITIVITY through their HARD WORK".
*"REAL FRIENDS are lie UMBRELLA,
We always find them in RAINY DAYS".
*"If you don't find a PLACE to
Stand that means you are the
FREE BIRD who can FLY HIGH".
****

Pratima Rai
M.Sc(B.Ed)
Kisahnganj, Bihar
*"WORKING in silence is the BEST WAY TO LEARN".
*SILENCE is good but SILENCING is DANGEROUS".
*"ATTITUDE is the REFLECTON of deeds".
*"ACCEPTANCES is the SIGN of NEW NORMAL".
*"YOU can do, WILLING to do and doing are the THREE
DIFFERENT
Versions of MAN".
****

-Author
Sakhi
Love, Nobility and Peace.
*"Life becomes EASY if you work for YOUR
Own SATISFACTION rather than PLEASING others".
*"When your ACHIEVEMENTS do some
FAVOUR of HUMANITY, it is SUCCESS".
*"LUCK is when PREPARATION meets OPPORTUNITY.
I have been CONTINUOSLY working and preparing myself for
attaining the BEST of TOMORROW.
The "BEST" is "YOU". I am hopeful of calling myself 'LUCKY'.
*"Don't get DISHEATENED if the WORLD treats you as an
OPTION.
You know you are the RIGHT ANSWER they are looking for.
Always VALUE YOUR PRESENCE'.
*"GREED for knowledge is FINE,
But knowing where and

How to use WISELY makes an
ULTIMATE DIFFERENCE".
*"Sparks of your SMILE can light up the
Darkest hour of a day for ANYONE who can
WITNESS your pure BEAUTY.
I am one of THEM".
*"Think of those moments where
You were PLEASED by beautiful
SOULS around you. Now it's time
To repay. Spread HAPPINESS and LOVE".
****

Bagmita Bhowmick
Radhakund, Mathura, Brindavan
B.Sc(Chem)
The view from the MOUNTAIN PEAK
Is same for all,
So, TRAINED your MIND to be like
The mountain so that it FINDS
NO DIFFERENCE.
****

CHAPTER FOUR

SPECIAL MESSAGE

Dear Students,

Life is hard and hard doesn't mean impossible!

It has always been tough for me to express myself. But when I see myself now, speaking in front of the camera without being conscious is where I believe, if you firmly and sincerely determine on doing or becoming something, you can.

Today I work as a Channel Mentor and Anchor for a News channel. But if I see the journey, it has real rise and falls, and when I say that, trust me they were really hard to take in.

Coming from a background of middle class family, with father being the only earning member, life is tough. It was tough to even think of pursuing our interests or passions, because these terms were too fancy for us at times. I being a bright student in school, was always expected to excel in everything I do, academics, co-curriculum (I am hardcore singer by the way), family values and what not. Everybody told me that I shall become a doctor or an engineer, some even thought I would end up being a scientist, really. Being clueless on what I would do in life I took science as in higher classes and started believing that I would be an engineer. Days went by and I started panicking a lot, thinking of what next?

After failing to clear JEE in the very first attempt, I understood this is not for me. I did my graduation in Chemistry, I thought maybe this is my calling, but maybe I chose the wrong university to pursue it. There was a huge language gap which literally destroyed my college life. Somehow I managed to not flunk and completed my degree but one thing was clear in my head that this is too is not meant for me. I don't fit in here.

Since my school days I was very shy but I was a confident person when it came to talk in my comfort zone. I loved talking and preaching people, for that matter. I enjoyed speaking in front of the masses in my excelled genres or areas. I always wanted to be someone who is heard by the masses. I wanted to reach out to people in need. I wanted to make people aware of things that are important in the society. But, I was clueless on how exactly to do so?

And then out of nowhere came this suggestion from my elder sister about Mass Media studies. In the beginning I didn't know what exactly it is but after doing a lot of research i was confident that I want to do this only. Then what, I applied for the course, i sat for the entrance and I cleared it in the very first go. This time it went so effortlessly unlike earlier when I sat for JEE entrance, may be because I wanted to do this from my heart and not because of external pressures.

It was bit of a shocker to my parents when I first revealed about my interest in the field. Their first reaction was, what is the point of putting in so much of efforts with science when you want to end up with arts. I had to make them realize that it's not about what stream you take, it is about how well you do in whatever field you are in. And finally I pursued my Post Graduation in Mass Communication from Sikkim Central University. It was a financial challenge to my family but then it went, something or the other was always managed and it went pretty well. I learned a lot in that course of 2 years. I not only learned new skills in mass communication, Television Production, Film Making, Radio Production and many more exciting things but also big and important life lessons. When I came back home after the two year course with a lot of experience and highest scores in all the four semester, my parents were more than happy.

But the struggle didn't end here, it had just started. People had always criticized me for changing my field of subject from Science to Arts, and that I made a terrible mistake in life and that I have no future ahead in this field.

All these comments really were breaking my courage and positive affirmations that I had developed in last two years. I had no idea where to start from, how should I find a job, how am I going to compete with those extra ordinary candidates, what if I fail? Everywhere I was applying they were looking for experienced candidates and I was a raw, who would hire me anyways?, I saw some of my friends getting good opportunities with either by their contacts or work experiences and that was breaking my moral even more. I was all hopeless and was having second thoughts about maybe I made a bad decision in life.

And then I got a call from a News channel where I got an offer to work as a content writer, this lifted my confidence a bit and I did the job for a while but then again I realized writing is not my cup of tea, hence I quit it. Few days later, I got another call for a news anchor but I had to refuse that too because of the distance matters and the pandemic. Then I got a chance to do an internship as a social media manger, I liked the work as I got to learn a lot. Few days later to that, I got a call for an interview for a News channel again, and with least interest I went as I thought here also they would consider the experienced candidate over me. But to my surprise, they acknowledged my skills, my work, my understanding of the work and my dedication. They were so impressed with my approach that they hired me then and there.

Today, I'm a happily working news channel mentor and anchor. Being a fresher I'm given the liberty to experiment. Working in the fields has given me a lot of exposure to this outside world and how it functions. I may not earn a lot right now but this is a time when I'm preparing myself for the bigger pool out there. I'm polishing my skills, I'm learning every day, and I will keep learning, because learning has no end.

I am yet to achieve my goals but I have definitely started my journey towards it, step by step.

Problems are there and they will always be there, but this is our call on how we will handle it. If we won't take risks and face hardships now, then we would have enough to regret later.

Name: Shapna Chhetry

Designation: Channel Mentor & Anchor (Nepali devision)

R Voice News 24*7

Dear students

It's me Mr. Rohit Limbu, I was born in 0ctober 1988. I grew up in a middle class family. My father is an ex- Indian army, my hero and the source of motivation for me.I was grown up in an army cantonment area till I was 13 years old. I was in class 7th, when my father retired from his service.

Soon after my father's retirement, we had to face many hardships in our life.

Firstly, I was still a kid and was not matured enough, to understand the world.

Secondly, I felt completely lost when I was exposed to a completely new environment as life was different here from the cantonment zone.

We rented a house for more than 6 months, as our house was not completed. Our family now was completely dependent on my father's pension. We were bankrupt my father was chasing for loan, and my mother was bound to ask for money from our neighbors. I still remember my mother broke her piggybank (coin container) to feed us. Though my parents were suffering they always remain cool and calm and always kept a positive attitude. Finally after couple of months of ups and downs we were shifted to our own house.

Time passed, now I was in class-8 and I met Ranjan, a calm and quite boy. He was shy and a brilliant student among us. We used to tease him, as he was a shy boy. We were together till class-10. He passed the examination with good marks, and decided to choose science whereas I choose Humanities.

I still remember those class-10 board exams, I guess today's students still feel the same as I did, as it's the hardest part of our school life. As our class-10 results will decide our future.

''My marks don't make me laugh, but bunking classes makes me laugh''.

I had a late friend Mani; he was the man behind my class-10 results. I was very weak in math and still am. We studied all day long before our math board exam. His was pretty good in math, later he joined commerce but died at the age of 16.

Time flies now it was time for class-12 board exams. As you know by now that I was a humanities student, but math came to my life again through economics. This time I even took tuitions' for economics but it was still beyond my grab.

I still remember a funny incident all of us planned a picnic to celebrate New Year, and how we managed the picnic was really a thing not to be done by anyone; we used the tuitions' fees of economics for the picnic thanks to Mr. Rohit for the idea.

I failed in class-12 economics board exams twice. I passed economics after 2nd attempt and the score was only 37 when I passed it in my 3rd attempt. I was happy that I won against it. I had no pressure from family, they were happy for me.

Finally, I went to Nepal for British Army selection; I failed twice in the British Army selection and here also I succeeded in my third attempt. No pressure from family till I got selected in to the British Army, my family paid all my expenses. I had no idea till I got selected into the British army how my family managed to pay all my expenses. Today I am living my life; I got my family and love of my life. I am a married man now. When I look back at those days, it haunts me for few mistakes that I did.I would just say, "Don't worry about your future, it will ruin your present"

I would like to recommend some books, which will help you in future.

''Ikigai'' by Hector Garcia and Francesc Miralles, ''Dare to Lead'' by Brene Brown, and ''Think like a monk'' by Jay Shetty.

I would like to thank my family and friends for their infinite support and patience that they have shown by always being by my side.

And a big thank you to my dear friend Ranjan Thapa for giving me an opportunity to share my life story through his book. May God bless him!

I will leave you with few quotes that have inspired me over the years; they might help and inspire you too;

''Work hard when no one can see you''.

"It is better to be a man of value, than a man of success".

Thank you and good luck.
Name: Rohit Limbu
Designation: Soldier
Company: British Army
Dear Student,
My Name is Richa Upadhyay, from SIliguri (W.B) and I am working as a Marketing Analyst at IBM.

As we know very well, there is no scope for software engineers in Siliguri, and it was really challenging for me to choose this field. Well I was determined and wanted to look for career options in this field, so I had to move to Bengaluru because of the lack of opportunities here. After struggling hard for around 2years I was able to crack the interview in IBM. Before I got the job I was alone and sometimes felt very lonely too, but I never gave up as I had decided to prove myself and this was the driving force for me whenever I happened to lose hope or doubt my capabilities. I always admired and tried to learn from people who are well settled and successful in their career.

I got the opportunity to meet them and learnt a lot from them, some became my colleagues some became my good friends.in the journey of my life I have learned that if we decide to achieve something genuinely we are definitely going to get it. When one begins a journey many obstacles, ups and downs come into life but these should not break the desire to achieve ones dream one must keep on trying and should not lose hope as right thing happens at the right moment. The Important thing that I learnt from my Career is "Never Give Up" and would say the same to you, "Never doubt yourself and never give up."
Name: Richa Upadhyay
Designation: Marketing Analyst
Company: HBV/SIT/IBM

We always want good things to happen but sad times bring lessons. Forget about the sadness and keep lessons to get going. Take the bliss of life and be grateful.

I end with a saying: **"Be with nature as much as you can**
Live consciously, have faith, have patience,
Keep hope and blossom, wherever you go"!
Name: Ambika
Profession: Asst. Teacher
School: Rungbee Jnanpith, High School

35

36

LIFE CHANGING THOUGHTS

Dear Students,

Dear Students,

May the Divine bless you with good health, peace and positive vibes. As a child our life is full of examinations and challenges, it might be focusing on studies, scoring good marks and choosing our career. Always remember that every single step of yours towards your life is a stepping stone towards your bright future, so be very careful while you decide to take your steps. We all know that tasty chapatti can be made only when the dough is perfectly made. Similarly, if you want to succeed in life be focused on the preparation of dough i.e; your hard work. The more you work hard the more successful you will be.

Life is full of opportunities and chances, it is we who have to decide and choose, so choose wisely. There will be times when we will be shaken up by the storms and struggles in life, but we should face it positively and come out of it victoriously. No matter what life throws at us all of us have the caliber to face and win over it. Always remember we are the King of our Kingdom, no one can control our life.

Every situation brings with it a hidden gift with it, it is we whose choice can make it a boon or curse. Your future is in your hand so work hard to make it brighter.

God Bless You! Loads of Love.

Name: Sanjeesha Chandel

Designation: Principal

School:

Dear Student,

Let me begin with a very inspiring short story titled, 'Are You a Thermostat?' by John Parankimalil. The story goes like this:

One day, in his class, the science teacher asked the students, "Do you know the difference between a thermometer and a thermostat?" The student kept silent. No one answered. The teacher then told them, "A thermometer measures the temperature, while a thermostat measures the temperature and does something about it. If the temperature is too high, a thermostat may shut off the heat.

If the temperature is too low, a thermostat may trigger the heat to turn on. While a thermometer is a passive tool, a thermostat is an active one. They both experience the temperature, but a thermostat responds." Story ends.

REFLECTION - Some people are like thermometers – they passively allow what may harm them to just happen. They have problems and difficulties. They believe there isn't anything that can be done about them. They feel helpless as they watch life happen. They accept life as it comes to them. Others are more like thermostats. When they are faced with difficulties, they kick into action. They believe that something can be done; a solution can be found. They respond. They make decisions. They go into motion. Troubles and difficulties are an inevitable part of life. The question is 'how do you respond to them? Should you stay content as a thermometer or trigger yourself into action like a thermostat and change things within and around yourself?'

Way back in the mid 80's, the turmoil and panic arising from the insurgency grasped the Darjeeling Hills. Situations were not very conducive for the normal functioning of schools and colleges. Educational institutions were shut down. Almost all the Lecturers from Kolkata decided to go back home. We students were left in a lurch. Even worse, the University was firm in holding the Examination as scheduled. No postponement. Left on our own, we were helpless. A ray of hope shone upon us when the Teacher-in-charge of the Departmental Library sensed our state of desperation and laid his trust allowing us to use the library while he was away. This trust was indeed the driving force that triggered the renewed sense of enthusiasm and confidence. It acted like a catalyst in motivating and gave us a purpose for a goal to achieve. Yes, will do it!! Reading the text and the reference books helped to get a deep insight into the subject. The motivation was now backed by an utmost sense of determination and interest. Graduated with flying colours. The crisis taught a life time lesson – the choice to be a *'thermostat' worked.*

Today when I look back, somewhere I feel that motivation without a purpose would have been both futile and unsustainable. Having a purpose — a clear idea of what you want in life is a prerequisite to staying motivated. It helps you to re-ignite the fire whenever you feel low. Purpose and motivation are complementary in nature. Your purpose fuels your motivation, and your motivation in turn helps you to achieve and live your purpose. Motivation alone cannot take you very far. Your purpose gives your life a strong foundation. Motivation acts as its pillars. It supports you on your journey. It helps you get through difficult times, adding on to the strength provided by the strong foundation of your purpose. Your motivation will fluctuate, but your purpose remains constant, helping you advance steadily. What motivation does is it shortens your journey and makes it more enjoyable, more worthwhile. So, to stay motivated you must first figure out and set your purpose, only then you will succeed.

"When a goal matters enough to a person, that person will find a way to accomplish what at first seemed impossible." - Nido Qubein

Name: Mr. Michael Dutta
Designation:Senior Subject Master
Department of Geography
School: St. Paul's School
Jalapahar, Darjeeling

Printed by Libri Plureos GmbH in Hamburg, Germany